Trouble at Our Doorstep:

Public Attitudes and Public Policy on Central America

by Mark Rovner

ROOSEVELT CENTER FOR AMERICAN POLICY STUDIES

ISBN: 0-913217-08-5
Library of Congress Card Catalog number 87-60420

First Roosevelt Center Books printing February, 1987

Printed in U.S.A.

Trouble at Our Doorstep:

**Public Attitudes and Public Policy
On Central America**

Table of Contents

INTRODUCTION

Policy towards Central America currently ranks among the top concerns of U.S. foreign policy. Armed struggles within Nicaragua and El Salvador, a deteriorating Central American economy, widespread human rights abuses, and increasing Soviet involvement in the region have raised Central America to this position of prominence.

As the United States struggles to define an appropriate role in Central America, U.S. public opinion is of great importance. What is the U.S. public's image of the region? How does the U.S. public regard the growing crisis in Central America? What do U.S. citizens think of the role their country is now playing in the region and the one it might play in the future? This report attempts to help answer those questions by presenting and analyzing the results of six focused group discussions -- focus groups -- conducted around the country between June 25 and July 22, 1986.

The Roosevelt Center conducted the focus groups as part of its ongoing program of helping U.S. citizens better understand and form judgments about the policy issues that face the United States today. As with other Roosevelt Center projects, the one on Central America aims to help average citizens learn the basics of the problem, make informed judgments about the policy choices that face the nation, and ultimately learn how to communicate those judgments to the leaders and decisionmakers who make and carry out U.S. Central America policy.

By conducting the focus groups, the Roosevelt Center hoped to discover the baseline of public attitudes, opinions and knowledge -- what opinion researchers call **the public starting point.** In addition, we sought to uncover any major **obstacles** that might prevent the public from fully understanding the Central America issue. In general, such obstacles can include deeply ingrained attitudes about some aspect of an issue (for example, the role of the Soviet Union), lack of interest in the issue, a sense of incompetence to deal with the issue, or fear of, or aversion to, facing the issue. Finally, the focus groups sought to explore citizens' attitudes toward key U.S. policy choices in the region.

A focus group is a cross between a public opinion poll and a "rap session." Ten to twelve randomly chosen individuals are recruited to participate, and are paid for their time. Each group is stratified to represent a good distribution according to sex, age, educational background, and and income level.

Each session lasts about two hours and is led by a trained focus group moderator. It is the moderator's job to ensure that all members of the group participate, that participants feel confident to express their views, and that sincere disagreements are voiced. Techniques employed during each group vary, and may include written quizzes, role-playing, and hypothetical or direct questions put to the group for consideration.

A computer printout of opinion polls conducted by the major pollsters since 1979 on the subject of Central America makes a stack of paper nearly four inches high. For the most part, those polls offer valuable insight into trends in public opinion on a narrow but important range of issues, such as public knowledge of and support for U.S. policy in El Salvador and Nicaragua. Most of the questions vary on the themes of: Do you know which side we are on? Do you agree with the Administration's handling of the issue?

The Roosevelt Center's focus group discussions were more far-ranging, exploring questions that included: Why should we care about what goes on in Central America? What do the Soviets want in Central America? If you were a guerrilla in a certain situation, what would you do?

By adding breadth of coverage and interaction among participants, focus groups have for years played an indispensable role in market and opinion research. Focus groups offer insights that polling cannot. A focus group gets behind the opinions and offers some insight into the logic -- or lack thereof -- by which participants draw their conclusions. Focus groups can measure the effect of new information on participants' attitudes. Participants frequently change their minds based on additional facts provided by the moderator or as a result of debate with other participants. Also, because of their open-ended nature, focus groups uncover issues of intense public concern that are not revealed through traditional polling.

Because of their unscientific nature, focus group findings are best viewed as **hypotheses,** educated theories that someone might wish to validate scientifically later, but which are substantially accurate portrayals of the broad contours -- if not the fine details -- of public attitudes toward this issue. This report contains the hypotheses derived from six focus groups on Central America conducted between June 25 and July 22, 1986 in the following cities: Rochester, NY; Denver, CO; Kansas City, MO; Atlanta, GA; Seattle, WA; and Phoenix, AZ. At the time these groups took place, Congress was debating whether to send $100 million in aid to the anti-government "contra" rebels in Nicaragua, and the issue was receiving considerable publicity in the national media.

Many of the major findings in this report were reconfirmed during focus groups on a broader set of topics conducted by the Roosevelt Center in January 1987. Those groups took place in Nashua, NH, and Davenport and Des Moines, IA.

The report is divided into four parts. Chapter One is an overview of key findings. Chapter Two presents findings about the public's knowledge of Central America in general and what it sees as the causes of unrest there. Chapter Three examines public notions of U.S. interests in Central America. Finally, Chapter Four presents tentative public judgments on certain real and hypothetical policy choices that participants were asked to make. A Summary of Findings is presented at the end. An appendix gives additional background information on the focus groups themselves.

The focus groups were designed and moderated by the Roosevelt Center Director of Design, Mark J. Rovner, who is also principal author of this report. Dr. Richard A. Nuccio, Director of Latin American and Caribbean Programs, played a continuing and substantial role as fount of knowledge, analyst, editor, and skeptic. Marta Tanenhaus, Shira Saperstein, and Linda Lowenthal provided valuable advice and insight into the results. We also gratefully acknowledge the patient help of Roosevelt Center staff members Christina Namerdy and Yvonne Christy.

I. OVERVIEW

It is a truism among the pollsters that Central America is an example of public ignorance and lack of interest in foreign affairs issues. They cite poll after poll in which only a small fraction of the public can answer such basic questions as whether the United States supports the government or the rebels in Nicaragua. These focus groups certainly confirmed a lack of factual knowledge. But more significantly, they revealed that behind that superficial ignorance lies a deep concern, bordering on anxiety, about what is happening in Central America and a willingness to grapple with the issues when they are presented in a comprehensible way. U.S. citizens are worried about their country's growing involvement in Central America, they are worried about Soviet and other powers' involvement in Central America, and they are frustrated by their inability to get a handle on what is going on there.

FINDING 1. *Americans are worried about Central America, but believe they do not understand the problem.*

Concern was high among participants about what is happening in Central America. "Why do we have to be involved there?" blurted several participants in response to the question, "What is the first thing you think of when someone mentions Central America?" "Another Vietnam," "Instability," "War," and "The Soviets" were among the most frequent responses. Concern rose to the level of anxiety for a number of participants, who expressed fear of what is happening in Central America coupled with frustration over not understanding the problem and not trusting the media or the U.S. government to enlighten them or show the way to a solution. "No one (including our government) knows who our friends and enemies are down there," commented a Denver woman. Her comment reflected a widespread belief that the public receives only fragmentary information about Central America, and that even U.S. decisionmakers may not have enough information -- or judgment -- to make intelligent decisions. "I always get the feeling I never am really going to know what the true picture is," complained a Rochester man.

While worried, many participants were not immediately eager to learn more about or to discuss Central America. "There's a million things every day... it's hard to know about everything," complained a Kansas City woman. People acknowledge that the issue is important but have not sought to educate themselves. An Atlanta woman, asked whether she would consider attending a one- to two-hour learning event on Central America, responded in the negative, saying, "I have priorities," and devoting that much time to the issue did not rank high enough. Eight of the 12 Atlanta participants agreed. The exception to a general lack of initial interest was the Rochester group, many of whom claimed to have been following the issue for some time. They noted that the media, including such talk shows as *Donahue,* had covered Central America closely in the months before the focus group was conducted (June 1986). (The Rochester group took place the day of a key vote by the House of Representatives to send aid to the anti-Sandinista contra rebels in Nicaragua.)

Given the basic level of worry, it is not surprising that interest in the details of the Central America issue rose dramatically over the course of each group, as participants sought a way to grapple with their concerns. "We all appear to have more background knowledge than we actually thought we did," said a Seattle woman at that group's closing. Participants in almost all of the groups expressed surprise at how involved they had become in the issue of Central America. Virtually all of the participants in all six cities said they wanted to learn more about Central America at the session's close.

FINDING 2. *People do not believe that they have access to enough information about Central America to make a judgment.*

People complained of sporadic and haphazard media coverage and distorted arguments made by all of the principal actors in the debate over Central American policy. "I find it very confusing to read the paper or hear the news... there are so many hot spots all over and it's hard to decipher what all this is about," complained a Kansas City woman.

Most participants also believe that they are being manipulated by the U.S. government and others who advocate certain policies toward Central America. "You're always getting conflicting propaganda from both sides," said a Rochester woman. Ten of the 11 participants in Kansas City agreed with the proposition that "No one is giving straight information about what is going on in Central America." The same group, by a vote of 9-2, found President Reagan to be the least unreliable source of information on the issue.[1]

FINDING 3. *Despite a lack of detailed knowledge, people are prepared to make common sense judgments about key issues in Central America once they have an opportunity to examine the facts.*

In contrast to focus groups conducted by the Roosevelt Center in 1985 on the issue of the spread of nuclear weapons, people in the Central America focus groups had no difficulty grappling with the issues at hand. While some people observed that the choices were difficult in the sense of deciding between conflicting values or making choices without adequate information, no one expressed the belief that the issues were intellectually too challenging to consider.

This is an important finding for those seeking to increase the public's role in the Central America debate. Past research has shown that for many issues, one of the largest obstacles to increasing thoughtful citizen participation is a sense of intellectual inadequacy, that "I'm not smart enough to understand the problem." The technicalities surrounding the spread of nuclear weapons are a case in point.[2] When the issues surrounding the Central America problem are presented in a straightforward way, this obstacle does not arise.

---

[1] This result was, of course, derived before the recent controversy over the sale of arms to Iran and the alleged transfer of part of the proceeds to the contras. According to most public opinion polls, this controversy has, at least temporarily, harmed the public's sense of the President's reliability.

[2] For more about public views of the proliferation issue, see **The Spread of Nuclear Weapons: The Public's View,** Roosevelt Center, 1986.

II. THE STATE OF THE PUBLIC'S KNOWLEDGE

One of the key purposes of focus group inquiry in the area of public policy education is to provide an assessment of what pollster Daniel Yankelovich calls "the public starting place." This refers to the initial set of assumptions, beliefs, and facts that members of the public already have about an issue. It includes not only the mass of information in a person's head, but also how the person is likely to process new information and the extent to which conclusions about aspects of the issue are firmly entrenched in the person's mind.

This chapter reports on the information base people bring to the Central America issue. How much do people know? What do people think Central America is like socially, economically, and politically?

FINDING 4. *The public is poorly informed about what is happening in Central America.*

In general, people can only name two or three of the countries in Central America, and cannot identify the major issues facing each country. When asked to name the countries in Central America, 11 of 12 Atlanta participants could name Nicaragua, seven knew of El Salvador, Honduras, and Costa Rica, and one knew of Guatemala.

Nicaragua obviously occupies a distinctive position. Perhaps because these groups were conducted around the time of a major Congressional debate over funding for the Nicaraguan rebels ("contras"), awareness of Nicaragua and of the contras was markedly higher than any other Central American issue. Even on Nicaragua, however, knowledge was quite sketchy. In Kansas City, for instance, participants were asked what Central American issue had been the subject of recent debate. Nine of 11 knew the issue involved aid to insurgent forces, but only three knew the country involved was Nicaragua. As with other issues, Rochester participants deviated from the norm here: all 11 knew some details about the debate over contra aid.

Participants displayed only slightly more awareness of local issues dealing with Central America. In Seattle, eight of the group's 12 participants knew of an upcoming vote to repeal the city's status as a sanctuary city for Central American refugees who have entered the country illegally. In Denver, half of the group's 12 participants knew of a recent local controversy over the participation of the Colorado National Guard in military exercises in Honduras.

This relative ignorance, so often the centerpiece of public opinion poll analyses done in this area, is a significant counterpart to the concern focus group participants expressed on the issue, as well as to their willingness to grapple with the key questions surrounding U.S. Central America policy. It suggests that the task of helping the public play a more active and constructive role in policymaking in this area must begin with basic education. Given the skepticism people have toward their present sources of information, this process of education will need to begin by winning the public's trust concerning veracity and lack of bias.

FINDING 5. *There is little awareness of the debate within the United States over Central America policy.*

In general, people are not attuned to the debate within the United States over Central America policy. (The exception, at least at the time the focus groups were conducted, is policy on Nicaragua.) Moreover, people do not seem to have a sense that U.S. policymakers and activist groups are bitterly divided over Central America policy.

The latter point conflicts with the widespread view among policymakers and advocates that domestic politics over the Central America issue are polarized and hostile. In Seattle, we asked participants whether they sensed that the political debate over Central America seemed so. No one expressed that belief, despite indications we gained elsewhere that Seattle, like most places in this country, suffers from a highly divided and vitriolic political debate over Central America. The campaign to revoke the city's sanctuary status, according to local activists with whom we spoke, promised to be bitterly fought.

Low awareness of the domestic political debate represents both good and bad news for those seeking to engage the public on this issue. The bad news is that traditional methods of consciousness-raising, practiced by advocacy groups across the spectrum of viewpoints on the Central America issue, do not appear to have been successful in penetrating very far into the population. Promoting awareness among a significant segment of the population therefore may be a formidable task. The good news is that the concern expressed by some educators and political observers that the ugliness of the domestic debate has been a serious obstacle to involvement by thoughtful citizens may be unfounded.

FINDING 6. *People believe that Central America is socially and economically stratified, with widespread poverty, great wealth, and little middle class.*

When asked what Central American society was like, most participants painted a picture differing markedly from the United States, one fairly comparable to the picture painted by scholars and other experts. Participants consistently offered the opinion that in most Central American countries the vast majority of people are either very rich or very poor, and most are very poor. Participants' stereotypes of the Central American poor focused more on urban than rural poverty. Several participants expressed the belief that many of the wealthy in Central America derive their income from drug trafficking.

Participants suggested that the absence of a middle class was a major source of instability in the region. In truth, a small middle class has begun to develop in many of the countries in Central America, and many Central American scholars believe that the demands for change posed by that new middle class sparked the present wave of unrest in the region. This was one of the most fundamental points of discordance between the focus group participants and the prevailing expert view of Central American affairs.

Many participants viewed Central American culture as totally alien and, therefore, difficult to evaluate through North American eyes. Central Americans, these people say, are primitive, violent, and place less value on human life than North Americans. "Rich and poor have no meaning, [because] their culture is so different," said a Denver man. In a similar vein, a Kansas City woman agreed, remarking that, "the people that are running the governments just don't care about human life like we do." "[T]he different tribes in a lot of [Central American] countries are not as highly civilized as ours...they're always fighting," observed an Atlanta woman. "I'm not condemning the Central American people," said a Phoenix man, "but those people do not wish to work very diligently... They take their siestas every afternoon -- why do they do this? If those people would get off their ass and work there wouldn't be any of these problems."

Others saw the differences between North and Central America in a more sympathetic vein. Several participants indicated that the poverty and suffering that plague Central American are on a scale unmatched in the United States. One Denver woman, recounting a story of her own hardships many years ago, concluded, "I thought I was poor then, but I wasn't poor compared to the people down there [in Central America]." Another Denver participant reflected not only on the poverty in Central America but the near certainty that the poor will remain that way. "It must be a terribly hopeless kind of feeling to know they can't ever better themselves and that your children are never going to have more than you, which is nothing."

FINDING 7. *People associate Central America with poverty and war.*

Participants were asked to write down the first things they thought of when they thought about conditions in Central American countries. Responses overwhelmingly dwelt on conditions such as poverty, political instability, and bloodshed. (The next most common theme was beaches, vacation resorts, or retirement sites.) Most people could not add specifics to these overall impressions. Many knew that Nicaragua was a hot spot, but very few knew without prompting that El Salvador dominated front page headlines only a few years ago. Underlying this was a notion frequently raised by participants that Central Americans are inherently more violent than their neighbors to the North. "The biggest problem is that [both sides] have a terrorist mentality... conditioned by generation after generation of fighting," said a Kansas City woman.

FINDING 8. *People see the causes of unrest in Central America as an inextricable combination of internal and external factors.*

Participants were asked why they thought there was so much violence, war, and bloodshed in Central America. We were particularly interested in whether people saw the unrest in Central America as caused by internal forces such as economic inequality, or by external forces such as a superpower competition for influence and access. The public's response was quite sophisticated.

As cited above, people see the primary internal sources of tension as the disparity between rich and poor. These tensions, participants said, are aggravated by power struggles among vying factions within Central America. These internal struggles are in turn exacerbated by external intervention by outside powers, particularly the Soviet Union and the United States. Participants saw these factors as feeding on one another, and refused to rank order them when given the opportunity. In Atlanta, participants were given a list of possible sources of unrest and asked which was the most important. "It's all of them!" several replied, almost in unison.

While believing that no one root cause can explain Central America's political turbulence, many participants said that the near-term cause has been superpower politics. "Right now, the King and Queen are on the chess board and the others can't do a thing about it...they have no control over their destiny. It's a lot of superpower egos...it's a game, it's a joke," said an Atlanta man.

The public's view of the causes of unrest in Central America tracks very closely that of the experts. The experts would add only the escalating political and economic demands of a nascent middle class and the dominant tradition of repressive and reactionary government by the elites and the military.

FINDING 9. *People have a limited sense of some key actors in Central America and lack knowledge about the present and historical relationship between the United States and the region.*

There was virtually no unprompted mention of either the Catholic Church or the military in participants' depiction of Central American society. Both institutions play a significant role in Central American culture and politics.

People also have little sense of past U.S. involvement in Central America. Many participants do see continuing U.S. economic interests in Central America, particularly agricultural ones, despite the fact that U.S. economic investment in Central America has declined sharply in recent decades. Participant notions of U.S. economic interests seemed to reflect the once significant involvement of North American businesses in coffee, bananas, and other agricultural products that prevailed earlier in the twentieth century. One Denver participant expressed the correct belief that

Central America was an important cheap labor pool for assembling American electronics components.

No participants were aware of the long history of U.S. military invasions or one-time U.S. political control of many of the countries. Most frequently cited examples of past U.S. involvement in the hemisphere -- the 1983 Grenada invasion, the 1962 Bay of Pigs invasion of Cuba, and, in one or two instances, the 1965 occupation of the Dominican Republic by U.S. and other Latin American troops -- did not involve Central American countries.

We also asked Kansas City and Atlanta participants what they supposed Central Americans thought of the United States. In Kansas City, participants expressed the belief that most Central Americans are too involved in the daily struggle for survival to think of us at all. In Atlanta, participants suggested that many Central Americans might be resentful and hostile toward the United States, and that the disparities in wealth between the regions were a major source of those feelings.

III. PUBLIC VIEWS ABOUT U.S. INTERESTS

This chapter goes beyond the question of "What is going on down there?" to the next logical point of inquiry -- "Should we care about what is going on there and if so, why?" This chapter explores participants' perceptions of U.S. interests in Central America.

FINDING 10. *People are particularly concerned about the spread of Soviet influence in the region.*

Participants cited the Soviets as their single largest source of concern in Central America. This concern was in part because the Soviets represent a threat to U.S. authority in the region and in part out of fear of the spread of Soviet communism. Most participants did not express fear of a direct Soviet threat to the United States using Central America as a base. Some participants were aware of the possibility of a Soviet missile threat from the region. But while one or two participants cited fears of a Soviet-sponsored invasion of the United States from the south, several explicitly discounted it.

In Denver, seven of 12 participants said that keeping the Soviets or any other foreign power out of Central America is the main U.S. concern in the region. "The Russians are just like... a cancer. They'll start and just grow and grow, gradually, not overnight, but over a period of years," said a Kansas City man. A Phoenix woman expressed concern that, "Having them take control so close to home would make me a little nervous."

Not all participants saw Soviet influence as a major threat, and most people concluded that the Soviets are more interested in distracting the United States than they are in actually expanding into the region. (See Finding 11, below.) People are nonetheless worried enough to support taking steps to diminish or prevent Soviet influence in Central America.

The public's willingness to be involved, however, does not automatically translate into support for present U.S. policies. Public ambivalence toward the Administration's contra policy in Nicaragua is a case-in-point. (See Finding 20.)

Two outspoken and self-proclaimed conservatives, in Atlanta and Phoenix, voiced the strongest arguments against worrying about Soviet involvement in Central America. The Atlanta man summed up his position with the observation that, "Soviet missiles in Warsaw [sic] are just as accurate as they would be from Managua, Nicaragua." The Phoenix man (who described himself at the end of the discussion as "so conservative and so Republican it's pitiful") said: "The only reason Russia hasn't taken over is because they feel they can't take over because we'll nail them before they can nail us. I don't want to see the Russians down there, but for goodness sake, if they want to go down there--hell, let 'em have it... What have they got in Cuba? Hell, they can't even grow decent tobacco anymore...."

While reasonably clear in their positions on the Soviets, participants were inconsistent in their opinions on communism. Most expressed clear opposition to communism, socialism, or Marxism-Leninism yet, when asked, had little idea what those terms mean. In particular, participants could not agree on what "communism" was. In Phoenix, where this question was explored further, some participants stressed that an undemocratic, dictatorial system was at the core of what they saw as "communist." Others cited lack of private property or, in the words of a Phoenix woman, "a welfare system where everyone's equal...where everything belongs to the government."

FINDING 11. *After some reflection, people believe that Soviet interest in Central America is probably limited.*

Participants, while concerned about Soviet involvement in Central America, saw the Soviet role in the region as, in the words of a Rochester woman, "interested in starting a little agitation here, a little agitation there." She continued, "They might be hoping to divert the United States' attention from other things they might have up their sleeves that would be worse in the long run." Her fellow participants agreed: eight out of 11 people in the Rochester group said they thought Central America was "a low priority" for the Soviet Union (one said it was probably a high priority). The Rochester group was given a hypothetical situation in which they were advisors to General Secretary Gorbachev, who announces that the Sandinistas are in danger of losing power unless the Soviets send their own troops in. By a vote of 10 to 1 the group agreed that the Soviets would be unlikely to send troops, though they might send large amounts of aid and encourage the Cubans to go in as their proxies. (It bears noting that the Rochester group was no more or less liberal than the other focus groups. In fact, the President's Nicaragua policy received more support from this group than from any other.)

This notion prevailed in all of the groups in which it was discussed. In Seattle, one participant explained that geography necessarily made Central America a second-level priority for the Soviets. "[The United States] can do [to] Central America just like Russia can do to Central Europe," he explained. (It is, however, also worth noting that participants did not generally believe the United States should behave in this way. See Findings 17 & 19.) In Seattle and elsewhere, as participants discussed the Soviet threat among themselves, the consensus emerged that Soviet motives in Central America were more to be a "bee in the U.S. bonnet" than to acquire a launching platform for an attack or invasion of the United States.

FINDING 12. *People are concerned about creating "another Vietnam."*

Some participants expressed concern about the United States becoming embroiled in a long war involving U.S. troops, as happened in Vietnam. Most participants, including those who supported U.S. involvement of some sort, believe military involvement is unnecessary at best, and foolhardy at worst. Perhaps not surprisingly, the strongest concern was expressed by a Phoenix man in his late teens: "I'm that age group where I'd get to go over there, which I wouldn't mind doing for the cause, but it'd be a stupid one... just like Vietnam was." Others were prepared to overcome their reluctance: "It would be unfortunate to have any young men lose their lives, but that would save more lives because we can't afford to have people like that [communists] around here," said a Rochester woman.

FINDING 13. *People care about the deprivation and oppression that plague so many of the inhabitants of Central America, yet they are unprepared to commit U.S. resources for purely altruistic purposes.*

Participants of all political stripes generally supported a policy principle of only getting involved in Central America to the extent that it serves a direct U.S. interest. A number of participants voiced frequent, and sometimes impassioned, expressions of sympathy for the plight of many Central Americans (see Finding 6), most participants concluded--often in so many words--that "we are not our brother's keeper."

The minority view, that we should help Central Americans regardless of our interests, received its strongest support in Kansas City. "I think that the United States, because we are the United States, should be involved any place where we can successfully help, and I don't care how....," said one Kansas City woman.

FINDING 14. *Participants had little unprompted understanding of the "human rights" issue.*

The human rights issue was not a central element of our inquiry. To the extent we did explore it, however, we found a poorly developed sense of the issue among participants.

In Kansas City, five of 11 participants had never heard of the term "human rights." When told that "human rights" refers to basic due process and political protections that are central features of our political system, many participants argued that the "differentness" of Central American society made these issues less relevant. The following views of a Rochester woman reflect that belief: "We have all been brought up with different values and different lifestyles than those people and they never are really going to understand. We can tell them about the pursuit of happiness and they are never going to have the funds to understand where we are coming from anyway."

Those who were familiar with the human rights issue differed over its importance. In Rochester, where understanding of the issue ran higher than in other groups, some argued strongly that the United States should make human rights a policy priority. "If we pride ourselves as a nation on human rights, how can you turn a deaf ear to people who are asking for help, especially when they're right on your doorstep?" asked one woman. A man from the same group cited self-interest for his emphasis on human rights: "The more countries... that don't care about... individual dignity and liberty, the more threat we have in the United States of losing it." Other views reflected the more generally held notion that U.S. involvement required a direct U.S. interest (See Finding 19).

FINDING 15. *Some people are concerned about the impact of Central America's problems on illegal immigration to the Untied States.*

A handful of participants expressed concern about the effect the turmoil in Central America was having on illegal immigration to the United States. Typical among these concerns was that of a Phoenix man: "We have so many countries down south of our borders that can be taken over like Cuba was that the more Russian borders will get closer to home, the more problems we're going to have... and because of the expansion of Soviet bases it's going to cause... a lot of national problems with immigrants coming in..." Not surprisingly, these concerns were largely limited to Phoenix and Denver, both of which receive a significant influx of Latin American immigrants, both legal and illegal.

IV. PUBLIC JUDGMENTS ABOUT U.S. POLICY IN CENTRAL AMERICA

The final line of inquiry in the focus groups involved asking people what the United States should do about Central America in light of what is happening there and in light of U.S. interests. These questions were explored both through direct questioning and, in later groups, by having participants play the role of different players in a variety of situations. We were interested not only in specific choices, such as aid to the Nicaraguan contra rebels, but also in people's decisionmaking principles, general notions of how the United States should behave, and what factors are relevant to making a decision.

FINDING 16. *People believe we have no choice but to be involved in Central America.*

Most participants, while concerned about the expenditure of money abroad and the risks of military involvement, support U.S. involvement in Central America. This support rose during the course of each group as participants became more familiar with the issues.

"It's our neighborhood!" said a Denver participant, summing up the consensus in all six cities that the geographical proximity of Central America gave it special significance. In Kansas City, all 11 participants agreed that the United States should be involved in Central America. In Seattle, seven of ten agreed that the United States should be involved. In Denver, ten of 12 expressed that belief.

In almost every case, the presence of the Soviets was cited as the principal motivating factor for U.S. involvement. In Denver, participants acknowledged the Soviet issue but cited a broader concern. The goal should be to stop the Soviets in the short run, but keep *all* other foreign powers out as well.

As each group progressed, participants developed an increasingly sophisticated view of U.S. relations with Central America. "You can't say don't get involved. We *are* involved... [in many ways] there's no way to get *un*-involved," concluded a Seattle woman. "The world is too small a place for us to stick our heads in the sand..." said a Denver man.

At each group a minority consistently argued for a hands-off approach. Principal arguments against involvement included the futility of intervening in Central American affairs and the existence of higher priorities at home. "Let them fight," argued a Denver woman. "They've fought since the beginning of time and they'll fight to the end of time..." A Rochester woman concluded, "I think there are just too many problems in our own country right now without having to go spend our money down there."

FINDING 17. *People are hesitant to support direct U.S. military involvement in Central America.*

Most participants would not favor the use of U.S. troops unless a Soviet-sponsored communist nation in Central America invaded its non-communist neighbors. Even then, many would oppose direct U.S. military involvement.

In Atlanta, participants, by a two-to-one margin, voted to use U.S. troops only if there were a direct threat to the U.S. mainland. Given a scenario in which Cuba and Nicaragua had launched air invasions into Costa Rica and Honduras, only four of 12 believed the use of U.S. troops would be appropriate.

Rochester was the most "hawkish" of the six groups. There, participants were asked how many would support invasion in a scenario in which the Sandinistas had taken complete control of the country, the contras had been eliminated, and the Sandinistas were beginning to foment revolution in neighboring countries such as Honduras or Costa Rica. Six of the 11 were prepared to support invasion under those circumstances. A seventh indicated that he might support invasion if it were clear that the target countries were calling for U.S. help.

Those opposing direct involvement concluded that whatever our interests in Central America, they do not justify spending the lives of loved ones. A Rochester woman's concern was echoed at all groups: "In the background I continue to worry about losing North American lives as I have a young son and I picture him being involved in a situation like this and I would feel awful putting him in a situation like this."

This finding suggests that U.S. citizens have evolved beyond the strong isolationism that prevailed in the late 1970s following Vietnam. Participants consistently supported U.S. involvement in Central America and, by inference, elsewhere. Most people, however, still draw the line at sending in U.S. troops.

FINDING 18. *People believe that the United States should, in general, only take measures in Central America that directly serve U.S. interests.*

At a number of the groups, participants had an opportunity to choose among various objectives for U.S. policy in Central America. Helping the Central Americans consistently ranked behind other objectives that more directly served U.S. interests, such as stopping the Soviets or protecting U.S. economic interests.

In Seattle, for instance, of the seven participants who agreed that we should be involved in Central America only one cited the needs of the Central Americans themselves as the controlling reason. As noted earlier, humanitarian motives were supported by several Kansas City participants as well.

People may, however, be willing to extend their notion of what is in U.S. interests. For instance, a Rochester man argued that the United States should take an aggressive approach in favor of human rights because, by promoting minimum standards of due process as an international norm of political behavior, we would be helping to preserve it here. An Atlanta woman made a similar observation regarding the Soviets: "If you make sure that the economic situation improves down there... that also makes certain that when the Soviets come in and say, 'Here, I've got a dollar,' they say 'I don't need that dollar.'"

FINDING 19. *People remain concerned about unnecessary U.S. interference in the affairs of Central America.*

There are three strands to the line of argument that holds that the United States should "Let Central America Be Central America." The first is an aversion to any sort of U.S. involvement in the affairs of other countries for fear of getting sucked into foreign crises. The second is a belief that Central Americans should be able to choose how they wish to conduct their own affairs. The third is a belief that, whatever the motives, U.S.

interference in the affairs of other countries almost never works to our advantage or to theirs.

As noted, a minority of participants simply did not think we should get involved in other countries' problems. Far more concern, however, was expressed about U.S. usurpation of Central Americans' rights to control their own lives. "They've got to make their own decisions," said a Seattle man. "We're [wrongly] assuming that they're poor ignorant people and we have to show them the way," observed a woman at the same group. "Our dreams are not necessarily ... Nicaragua's dreams..." concluded a Kansas City woman.

Quite a few participants were cynical about whether U.S. policy would be constructive. "Maybe we have too grandiose ideas for the rest of the world, and maybe we shouldn't have so many of them. We want to do things differently, bigger, like we do it -- maybe we ought to let all of them think for themselves for a while. Maybe we're wrong," said an Atlanta woman.

These concerns were shared by many who on balance, ultimately, favored some level of U.S. involvement in Central America. A Rochester man's comment probably represents the consensus view: "...I agree [we should] let them decide what they want. But if what they want turns out to be a full communist state with missiles aimed at Rochester, New York, then all of a sudden charity begins at home...and they can all go to hell."

FINDING 20. *In general people support current policy toward the Nicaraguan rebels or "contras," but they are skeptical about it.*

In Rochester and Kansas City participants were given three choices: (1) Favor the President's current policy of gradually undermining the Sandinista regime by supporting a native rebellion (i.e. the contras); (2) Send U.S. troops to oust the Sandinistas right away; or (3) Do nothing. We told participants that: Choice 1 might or might not lead to a contra victory, but would probably take many years and cost thousands of Nicaraguan lives; Choice 2 would almost certainly succeed in installing a government friendly to us, but might cost as many as 2,000 American lives; and Choice 3 would almost certainly mean the end of the contras and solidification of Sandinista control of Nicaragua.

In Kansas City, eight of 11 chose current policy, i.e. Choice 1. In Rochester, five of 11 participants agreed. Four Rochester participants and no Kansas City participants chose the "do nothing" option.   Three Kansas City participants and two Rochester participants chose the invasion option.

While most frequently chosen, the option of support to the contras was not strongly defended.   Many participants admitted being caught between concern over the Soviet presence in Central America and a strong desire not to commit U.S. lives to the struggle.   Significantly, no participants discussed the Nicaraguan rebels in a favorable light.   There was no evidence that participants view them as heroes or freedom fighters or comparable to the U.S. founding fathers, as some contra supporters have argued.   The more typical defense of the contras came from a Kansas City woman who said: "If [the Sandinistas] claim to be Marxist-Leninist, we *know* what that's all about ...   Wiping them out would be what we'd focus on rather than [who would take over]." In addition to Rochester and Kansas City, participants raised the issue spontaneously in Atlanta and Phoenix.   Supporters and opponents of the contra policy shared some misgivings about this approach.   Chief among these concerns are the questions of who the contras really are and whether the money we send them is being properly spent.

"We supported Castro, and threw out Batista, and now look what we got... I don't want... to spend $100 million down there and just end up with another Castro," said an Atlanta man. Others expressed the opposite, more common concern that the contras would install a brutal right-wing dictatorship.   Another Atlanta participant raised the question of where the money is really going: "All this money and stuff that we send down there, is it getting to who it belongs to or is it ending up in a Swiss account like Marcos' did?"

Participants favoring the do-nothing option (Option 3) raised the above arguments and others.   "It seems to me like Reagan, his answer to fixing a problem is throwing more money at it, and I don't think that's the right way," said a Kansas City man. Others raised concerns about U.S. interference with the rights of countries to choose their own fate. "Aren't we doing the same thing the Soviets are doing?" worried a Phoenix man. "If we're going to start giving them [anti–Communist rebels] money, aren't we inflicting our ideas on them and doing the same thing the Soviets are doing when they come in and say you have to do this and this?" "Who are we to go in there and do what we think is right? It's not our country," echoed a Rochester woman. Still others fell back on the issue of economic priorities: "That $100 million [in aid to the contras] could feed a lot of hungry people," said a Rochester woman. "I worry about the threat of communism too, but I'd feed my family before I'd give to [anti-communist rebels]."

Proponents of the invasion option accepted the need for action, but rejected the contra option as an inadequate step. "If we're gonna go to war, let's go to war and get it over with and not play games... The Soviet Union is expanding just like Hitler did...   Either quit playing games or go the heck to war," argued a Kansas City man. "I can't see where you hand them money and let it go at that. If you are worried about the threat, you go all the way or you don't go," echoed a Rochester man. Another Rochester man likened the contra policy to "putting a bandaid on a cut that runs all the way up your arm. Then if it gets worse you put a new bandaid on. Why not just put stitches up the whole thing to begin with?"

Other participants, including self-described conservatives, argued that our quarrel is not with Nicaragua but with the Soviet Union. "Sometimes it seems that it's not really Nicaragua that we're concerned with -- it's the Soviet Union and the United States are giving [aid] back and forth ... it's more like Nicaragua's a toy," said a Rochester man. A Phoenix man took this view to its ultimate conclusion: "Why pick on the little people? Why not go after the country that started the problem? Either start a war with Russia or get the hell out."

Further evidence of the fragility of the majority's support for the existing policy of U.S. aid to the Nicaraguan contra rebels came in Seattle and Atlanta, where participants were asked to act as U.S. decisionmakers facing a crisis in a "hypothetical" Central American country. The hypothetical country was described as a democratic revolution-gone-sour: A despotic dictator was overthrown five years ago. The new regime immediately expropriated much land and property belonging to the old oligarchs. Five years later, the regime had proclaimed itself "Marxist-Leninist" and begun to abridge rights of free speech and other civil rights. There were increasing contacts with the Soviets.

Decisionmakers (i.e., the participants) had to decide on a request by a group of rebels seeking aid to help topple the new regime. In Seattle, participants voted 8-2 *against* helping the rebels. In Atlanta, not a single participant voted to support the rebels. In both Atlanta and Seattle, the strongest argument against aiding the rebels was not trusting the rebels themselves. "No matter how much money we put in," said a Seattle man, "how many successful true democratic societies have been set up? The only time these people are friends to us is when we have something they want."

---

[1] This finding, too, may be affected by the recent controversy over U.S. arms sales to Iran and alleged diversion of funds to the contras.

SUMMARY OF FINDINGS

CHAPTER I -- KEY FINDINGS

FINDING 1. Americans are worried about Central America but believe they do not understand the problem.

FINDING 2. People do not believe that they have access to enough credible information about Central America to make a judgment.

FINDING 3. Despite a lack of detailed knowledge, people are prepared to make common sense judgments about key issues in Central America once they have an opportunity to examine the facts.

CHAPTER II -- THE STATE OF THE PUBLIC'S KNOWLEDGE

FINDING 4. The public is poorly informed about the details of what is happening in Central America.

FINDING 5. There is little awareness of the debate within the United States over Central America policy.

FINDING 6. People believe that Central America is socially and economically stratified, with widespread poverty, great wealth, and little middle class.

FINDING 7. People associate Central America with poverty and war.

FINDING 8. People see the causes of unrest in Central America as an inextricable combination of internal and external factors.

FINDING 9. People have a limited sense of some key actors in Central America, and lack knowledge about the present and historical relationship between the United States and the region.

CHAPTER III -- PUBLIC VIEWS ABOUT U.S. INTERESTS

FINDING 10. People are particularly concerned about the spread of Soviet influence in the region.

FINDING 11. After some reflection, people believe that Soviet interest in Central America is probably limited.

FINDING 12. People are concerned about creating "another Vietnam."

FINDING 13. People care about the deprivation and oppression that plague so many of the inhabitants of the region, yet are unprepared to commit U.S. resources for purely altruistic purposes.

FINDING 14. People have almost no unprompted understanding of the "human rights" issue.

FINDING 15. Some people are concerned about the impact of Central America's problems on illegal immigration to the United States.

CHAPTER IV -- PUBLIC JUDGMENTS ABOUT U.S. POLICY

FINDING 16. People believe we have no choice but to be involved in Central America.

FINDING 17. People are hesitant to support direct U.S. military involvement in Central America.

FINDING 18. People believe that the United States should, in general, only take measures in Central America that directly serve U.S. interests.

FINDING 19. People remain concerned about unnecessary U.S. interference in the affairs of Central America.

FINDING 20. People in general support current policy toward the Nicaraguan rebels or "contras," but they are skeptical.

FOCUS GROUP SCHEDULE

City	Date	No. of Participants
Rochester, NY	6/25/86	11
Denver, CO	6/30/86	12
Kansas City, MO	7/1/86	11
Seattle, WA	7/14/86	10
Atlanta, GA	7/21/86	12
Phoenix, AZ	7/22/86	11